MIA
HAMM

MIA

HAMM

CARL EMERSON

THE CHILD'S WORLD®, INC.

ON THE COVER...

Front cover: Mia concentrates on a loose ball during a 1998 game.
Page 2: Mia smiles to the crowd after a 1997 game against Canada.

Library of Congress Cataloging-in-Publication Data
Emerson, Carl.
Mia Hamm / by Carl Emerson.
p. cm.
Includes index.
ISBN 1-56766-829-1 (lib. reinforced. : alk. paper)
1. Hamm, Mia, 1972——Juvenile literature.
2. Soccer players—United States—Biography—Juvenile literature.
3. Women soccer players—United States—Biography—Juvenile literature.
[1. Hamm, Mia, 1972– 2. Soccer players. 3. Women—Biography.]   I. Title.
GV942.7.H27 E64 2000
796.334'092—dc21
00-038339

PHOTO CREDITS

© AP/Wide World Photos: 6, 10, 16, 19, 20, 22
© Bongarts Photography/SportsChrome-USA: 9
© Rob Tringali, Jr./SportsChrome-USA: cover, 2, 13, 15

TABLE OF CONTENTS

ON TOP OF THE WORLD

In 1999, the Women's World Cup was played in the United States for the first time. The U.S. team had been a power in women's soccer for years, but this year was different. This was a chance to showcase their sport—and women's sports in general—to the people of the United States. Games in the **tournament** would be played all over the country. The U.S. team's games were being shown on national cable television. When the team made it to the championship game, it was broadcast on national television.

Almost 100,000 people showed up at the Rose Bowl in California to watch the game. Many of them waved American flags and had their faces painted red, white, and blue. They screamed for the U.S. team. In the middle of it all was Mia Hamm. Mia is one of the best women's soccer players in history. In fact, she has scored more goals than any other woman in **international** competition.

The U.S. played China in the final **match.** It was a hard-fought game, and both teams had great chances to score. But at the end of regulation time, the score was still 0–0. Neither team scored in the overtime, either. So, the game had to go to a **shootout.** In a shootout, each team has five different players attempt a **penalty shot.** Whichever team scored the most would win.

Mia (jumping) celebrates with her teammates after kicking a penalty shot against China on July 10, 1999.

Penalty shots are very hard for a goalie to stop. Both teams' players were making them easily. Mia was one of the players selected to shoot, and she made her shot. Finally, the U.S. goalie, Brianna Scurry, stopped one of the Chinese shots. When Brandi Chastain made the last U.S. kick, the U.S. team had won. Mia and her teammates were champions once again—this time in front of thousands of screaming fans and millions more watching on television. It was a special moment for women's sports.

LEARNING THE GAME

Mia was born in Selma, Alabama on March 17, 1972. Her real name is Mariel Margaret Hamm. Her mother called her Mia because she reminded her of a ballet teacher who had that name. Because Mia's father was in the military, her family moved around a lot. Before she even turned 2, she learned to love soccer. Her family lived in Italy, where soccer is the main sport. She loved to watch the players handle the ball with their feet with such great control. The more her family watched the game, the more they loved it.

When they moved back to the U.S., they eventually settled in Wichita Falls, Texas. When she turned 5, Mia's parents signed her up for that city's youth soccer program. Mia was a shy girl, except when she was on the soccer field. Then, she was very aggressive. Even though she was one of the smallest and youngest players on the team, she was also one of the best.

Mia holds the Women's World Cup trophy after USA's win over China on July 10, 1999.

→

That same year, Mia's parents adopted a boy named Garrett. He was three years older than Mia, but they quickly became very close. Mia already had two older sisters and an older brother, but she and Garrett had a special relationship. Garrett let little Mia play with kids his age. Playing sports with older kids helped Mia improve her skills. But she didn't just play soccer. She played baseball and football too, on teams with boys. Even in junior high, she made the football team. While she was smaller than the other players, she was also faster. She played wide receiver and kicker. But soccer was her best sport.

Mia was a forward. She was faster than most of the other players, and she could handle the ball better. Sometimes, she would surprise her own teammates with a pass they didn't expect! When the other team had the ball, Mia always seemed to know where the ball was going before it got there. She was the best player at her high school in Wichita Falls. She was named to the Texas All-State team when she was just 13 years old.

At this time, women's sports were growing in popularity. Mia got the chance to play in some all-star games. John Cossaboon, who was coach of the U.S. Olympic development team, saw Mia play at one of these games. He couldn't believe she was so young! He asked her to join his team.

Mia works the ball during a practice session in New Jersey on June 17, 1999.

MIA GOES NATIONAL

Mia played for just one year on the Olympic development team. Coach Cossaboon saw how talented she was and recommended her to Anson Dorrance, the coach at the University of North Carolina. Coach Dorrance also coached the U.S. national team, and was considered to be one of the best coaches in all of women's soccer.

Coach Dorrance saw Mia's potential right away. He knew she still had a lot of learning to do about the game, but she was only 15. He knew she could one day be one of the best soccer players in the world—if she was willing to work at it. And he found out quickly that she was willing to work! Coach Dorrance was also trying to build a powerhouse national team. The World Cup was the world championship of men's soccer. He was certain that there would soon be a World Cup tournament for women.

Mia first started playing and practicing with the national team in 1987. That same year, her family moved to Virginia, and Mia was forced to switch high schools. She quickly made new friends and played on her high school team, a club team and the national team while she was still in high school. Mia was also a very good student. In fact, she graduated from high school a year ahead of schedule!

Mia battles for a loose ball during a game against Canada in 1997.

THE COLLEGE YEARS

Mia was named an All-American in high school, and Dorrance offered her a **scholarship** to attend the University of North Carolina. There, she played on the Tar Heels' women's soccer team, which was already a national power. Many of the members of the national team also played for North Carolina.

Adding Mia to the team only made the Tar Heels stronger. She proved to be one of the best players in the history of women's college soccer. Her lightning quickness, accurate shots, and pinpoint passes helped the Tar Heels win the national championship her first two years in college.

All the while, Mia continued to play on the national team. Midway through her college career, the first Women's World Cup was held in 1991. In order to play in the World Cup, Mia had to commit to the team for the year. That meant she had to leave college. It was a hard decision for her make. She was only 19 years old, and would be the youngest member of the team. Still, it was an opportunity she couldn't pass up.

The U.S. had a hard time getting ready for the World Cup. They weren't playing their best soccer when the tournament started. Mia had learned a new position, midfielder, where she had more defensive duties than she had ever had before. She was an excellent playmaker, though, and she handled the change well.

Mia keeps her eye on the ball during a 1997 game.

In the first round of the tournament, the U.S. survived a close 3–2 game against Sweden. No one expected the U.S. team to go very far, since other countries had national teams longer than the U.S. did. But the Americans kept advancing, and finally defeated Norway in the championship match, 2–1. They had surprised even themselves, and won the first Women's World Cup.

Mia returned to school in 1992 and again played for the Tar Heels. That year's team was perhaps the best in the history of college women's soccer. With Mia leading the way, North Carolina went 25–0 and again won the championship. Mia was named U.S. Soccer Female Athlete of the Year, and most valuable player of the national tournament. She led the nation in scoring. Obviously, her year on the national team had improved her skills even more.

In her last year in college, Mia again led the Tar Heels to the championship. She ended her college career as the all-time leading goal scorer in the tough Atlantic Coast Conference, with 103 goals. She also had the most **assists** (72) and the most points (278) in the conference's history. She received the Honda Broderick Cup as the most outstanding female athlete in collegiate sports. She was an All-American three times, and the University of North Carolina retired her uniform number, 19, in 1994.

Mia dribbles past Germany's Sandra Minnert during a Women's World Cup quarterfinals match on July 1, 1999.

HIGHS AND LOWS

The World Cup is played every four years. Mia was again on the 1995 World Cup team, but this time, the U.S. squad had a tougher time. They finished third, but Mia's strong play earned her the Most Valuable Player award.

The team was disappointed that they didn't win the World Cup, but they didn't have much time to feel sorry for themselves. The Olympics were just a year away. Mia and the rest of the team worked harder to make up for falling short in the World Cup. When the Olympics arrived in July of 1996, Mia and the team were ready. But this was a tough time for Mia. Back when she was in high school, her brother Garrett was diagnosed with a blood disease called **aplastic anemia.** Now his health was getting worse. Mia knew her brother loved to watch her play soccer. She was determined to play well for Garrett.

The team played well and made it to the championship game, in which they defeated China 2–1. They had won the gold medal! Afterward, Garrett hugged Mia and said, "I'm so proud of you." That meant more to Mia than the gold medal.

In 1999, the U.S. hosted the World Cup. Mia again led the squad. On May 22, she became the all-time leading scorer in international soccer when she scored her 108th goal. In July, the U.S. team regained the World Cup with that thrilling shootout victory over China.

Mia and South Korea's Yu Jin Kim chase the ball during the 1999 Nike Women's Cup.

HONORING GARRETT

Back in 1997, Garrett's health took a turn for the worse. He underwent a bone marrow transplant in February, but it couldn't save him and he died in April. To honor Garrett, Mia started the Mia Hamm Foundation, which raises money to help fight bone marrow diseases like aplastic anemia. Every year, she organizes the Garrett Game, a soccer game between national team members and top college players. The foundation has raised hundreds of thousands of dollars for research. Mia Hamm is a champion both on and off the field.

Mia signals to the crowd after USA's win over North Korea in the 1999 Women's World Cup.

TIMELINE

March 17, 1972	Mariel Margaret Hamm is born. Her mother calls her Mia.
1977	Mia signs up for soccer for the first time.
1985	Mia is named to the Texas All-State team.
1987	Mia joins the U.S. national team.
1989-90	Mia wins two national championships with the University of North Carolina.
1991	Mia leads the U.S. team to the World Cup championship.
1992-93	Mia leads North Carolina to two more national championships. She finishes her college career as the all-time leading scorer in the Atlantic Coast Conference.
1994	Mia's uniform number is retired at North Carolina.
1995	The U.S. team finishes third in the World Cup.
1996	Mia leads the U.S. team to the Olympic gold medal.
1997	Mia's brother, Garrett, dies of aplastic anemia.
May 22, 1999	Mia becomes the highest-scoring player in international soccer history with 108 goals.
July 10, 1999	Mia leads the U.S. to the World Cup championship.

Mia takes the ball past Sweden's Cecilia Sandell during their Algarve Cup match on March 16, 2000.

GLOSSARY

aplastic anemia (ay–PLAS–tic uh–NEE–mee–uh)
Aplastic anemia is a rare blood disease. Mia's brother Garrett died of aplastic anemia.

assists (uh–SISTS)
When a player passes the ball to another player who scores, it is called an assist. Mia scored many goals, but she also had many assists.

international (in–ter–NA–shun–ull)
Something that involves people from more than one country is called an international event. Mia has scored more goals in international competition than any other player.

match (MATCH)
Another name for a soccer game is match.

penalty shot (PEH–null–tee SHOT)
In a penalty shot, a player kicks the ball against a goalie from directly in front of the net. Mia made a penalty shot to help the U.S. win the 1999 World Cup.

scholarship (SKAH–ler–ship)
A scholarship is money given to a student to help pay for college. Mia got a scholarship to attend the University of North Carolina.

shootout (SHOOT–owt)
When each soccer team selects five players to attempt penalty kicks to decide a tie game, it is called a shootout. The U.S. national team won the 1999 Women's World Cup championship match in a shootout.

tournament (TUR–nah–ment)
A sporting competition that includes many competitors is called a tournament. Mia has led the U.S. national team to victory in many international tournaments.

INDEX